SCHOOL
Sawan
SERIES
Evolution Of The World
Social
Science
2
MANOJ PUBLICATIONS

Evolution of the world : Social Science – 2

Publisher :
MANOJ PUBLICATIONS
761, Main Road, Burari, Delhi-110084
Mobile : 09999476076, 09868112194
          08178823569, 08178854810
Email   : info@manojpublications.com
for online shopping visit our websites:
www.sawanonlinebookstore.com

ISBN : 978-93-5579-320-1

Contents

Our Food

Learning Points

- Kinds of Food
- Balanced Diet
- Sources of Food
- Meals of the Day
- Have Good Health

"Your diet is a bank account. Choices of good food are good investments."

– Bethenny Frankel

SPOTLIGHT

- Milk is called the complete food. It makes our bones strong. We make many products like cheese, butter, curd, sweets and ice cream from milk.

Food is our basic need. We need food to live. It helps us to grow and give us energy to work, play and think. It keeps us healthy and makes us strong.

KINDS OF FOOD

There are many kinds of food. They help us in different ways.

Evergy–Giving Foods

Foods like bread, chapatti, potato, rice, butter and nuts give us energy. Thereby, these are called the energy–giving foods.

Energy-giving foods

Body-Building Foods

Foods like pulses, eggs, meat, fish and milk help us to grow and make our bones and muscles strong. Thereby, these are called the body-building foods.

Body-building Foods

Protective Foods

Fruits and vegetables are protective foods. They help us to prevent diseases and keep us in good health.

Protective Foods

BALANCED DIET

Our diet is the food that we eat and drink regularly. A balanced diet includes the right amount of food from each food-group. It helps us to remain healthy.

SOURCES OF FOOD

You may think where food comes from. It comes from plants as well as animals.

We get fruits, vegetables, grains, nuts and oils from plants. We get eggs, milk and meat from animals.

We eat most food after cooking. But there are some foods like salad, fruit chaat, etc. which are eaten raw.

Salad

Fruit

MEALS OF THE DAY

A meal is the food that we eat at a particular time of the day. All of us mostly have three meals in a day. These are: breakfast, lunch and dinner.

Breakfast

It is the first meal of the day. We take it in the morning. The things that we take for breakfast are toast, butter, jam, idli, upma, puri, chapatti, cereals and eggs. It is the most important meal of the day.

Lunch

It is the second meal of the day. Usually we take rice, dal (pulses), chapatti, vegetables, meat, fish, curd, soup and salad at lunch. We take lunch at noon.

Dinner

It is the last meal of the day. Generally, we have it at night. Light dinner is good for health.

HAVE GOOD HEALTH

Follow these tips to have good health.

- ✓ Always take balanced food for good health.
- ✓ Always take fresh food.
- ✓ Do not waste food.
- ✓ Do not eat junk food.
- ✓ Do not eat much toffees and chocolates.
- ✓ Always take food in time.

Summary of the Chapter

- We eat food to live.
- We get food from plants and animals.
- Food makes our body strong.
- Three main meals are breakfast, lunch and dinner.

Raw: Uncooked
Breakfast: First meal of the day
Lunch: Meal eaten in the afternoon
Dinner: Last meal of the day

Evaluation Time

A. Fill up the blanks.

1. We get food from .... and ....
2. Some foods can be eaten ....
3. .... is the first meal of the day.
4. We eat most food after ....
5. .... makes our muscles strong.

B. Write T for a true statement and F for a false one.

1. Dinner is the first meal of the day.
2. Milk is not required for our growth.
3. Salad can be taken as raw food.
4. Wasting food is good.
5. Food is the source of energy.

C. Match the columns.

Column A	Column B
1. Butter	a. Helps in growth
2. Salad	b. Meals in a day
3. Light food	c. Lunch
4. Afternoon	d. Raw fruits and vegetables
5. Milk	e. Breakfast
6. Three	f. Dinner

D. **Name any three of each of the following.**

1. Energy-giving foods

   (i) ....   (ii) ....   (iii) ....

2. Body-building foods

   (i) ....   (ii) ....   (iii) ....

3. Protective foods

   (i) ....   (ii) ....   (iii) ....

E. **Answer these questions.**

1. Why do we need food?
2. Which foods do we get from plants?
3. Which foods do we get from animals?
4. How many meals do we have in a day?
5. What is a balanced diet?

Collect the pictures of the foods that can be eaten raw. Paste them on a chart paper and write their names. Out of these, encircle the ones that you like the most.

We should always eat clean and fresh food because food is the only way that gives strength to our body to do our work efficiently.

2 Water–Our Life

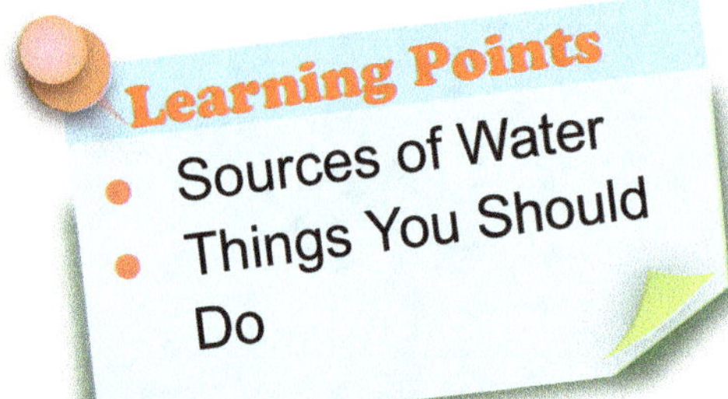

- Sources of Water
- Things You Should Do

> " Running water never grows stale, so you just have to keep on flowing."
> – Bruce Lee

SPOTLIGHT

- Water is very precious for us. We should not waste it.

All living things need water to sustain life.

We cannot live without water. Plants need water to make food. Humans and animals also need water to live. We need water for many other purposes. We need water to cook our food, wash utensils and clothes. We also need water to take a bath.

Animals need water

For Cooking

For Bathing

For Drinking

For Washing Clothes

For Gardening

For Washing a Car

For Boiling

For Filtering

SOURCES OF WATER

Rain is the main source of water. Rainwater collects in ponds, lakes, streams and rivers. Some rainwater goes into the ground. Ground water fills up wells. People use handpumps and tube-wells to draw out ground water.

Pond

Lake

Stream

River

Well

Tube-well

At home, we get water from taps and handpumps. Water may be pure or impure. We always need fresh and clean water to drink; otherwise, we may feel sick. We can get pure water by the process of boiling and filtering.

Boiling helps us to kill the germs in the water. Filtering helps us to remove the dirt in the water.

Boiling Water

Filtered Water

THINGS YOU SHOULD DO

- ✓ Always drink pure mineral water.
- ✓ Store drinking water in a clean pot.
- ✓ Keep drinking water covered.
- ✓ Do not waste drinking water.
- ✓ Always turn off the tap after use.
- ✓ Always keep water bodies clean.

Mineral Water

Summary of the Chapter

- We cannot live without water.
- We need water to drink, bathe, cook, wash and for other purposes.
- Rain is the main source of water.
- We should drink pure mineral water.
- We should not waste water.

Words to Know

Boiling: A method of heating water to kill germs

Filtering: A process of purifying water

Evaluation Time

A. Fill up the blanks.

1. Drinking dirty water makes us ....
2. We should drink .... water.
3. We should not .... water.
4. The main source of water is ....
5. When we are thirsty, we drink ....

B. Write **T** for a true statement and **F** for a false one.

1. Animals need water to live.
2. Seas are the source of water.
3. Plants do not need water to make food.
4. By boiling we get clean water.
5. At home, we get water from taps and handpumps.

C. Tick (✓) what is right and cross out (✗) what is wrong.

1. Reena throws away water for fun.
2. The taps in Simran's house are always leaking.
3. Ali always leaves drinking water uncovered.
4. Ravi turns off the tap as soon as the bucket is full.

D. Match the columns.

Column A	Column B
1. Rainwater	a. to do many things
2. We need water	b. main source of water
3. We must	c. helps us to kill germs
4. We cannot live	d. drink clean water
5. Boiling	e. without water

 Choose the words from the given box and write the correct use of water below each picture.

Cooking, Washing, Swimming, Drinking , Bathing

1. Watering Plants

2. ....

3. ....

4. ....

5. ....

6. ....

F.   Answer these questions.

1. Why do we need water?
2. For what other purposes do we need water?
3. What is the main source of water?
4. Where does rainwater collect?
5. How can we get pure drinking water?
6. How do people draw out ground water?
7. What would happen if we drank dirty water?
8. Differentiate between boiling and filtering.

A. Paste the pictures of the various sources of water in your scrapbook. Give heading "Water Sources".

B. Write a slogan on 'Save Water'.

If you see someone wasting water, how would you make him/her understand the value of water?

3 Our Clothes

- Clothes in Ancient Times
- Clothes in Modern Times
- Different Uniforms
- Things You Should Do

"Clothes mean nothing until someone lives in them."
— Marc Jacobs

SPOTLIGHT

- Clothes are one of our basic needs. They cover our bodies and make us feel better about ourselves.

Clothes are important to cover our bodies. They protect us from the sun, wind, rain, heat and cold.

There are varieties of clothes people wear in India. It depends on their regions, work and cultures.

CLOTHES IN ANCIENT TIMES

In ancient times, people covered their bodies with leaves, twigs and skins of animals. They were called aboriginals.

Aboriginal

CLOTHES IN MODERN TIMES

Unlike aboriginals, modern people wear modern clothes. In India, people wear different types of clothes in different seasons.

In summer, people wear cotton clothes which keep them cool. We get cotton from cotton plants.

In winter, people wear warm clothes. These clothes are mostly woollen. Most common woollen clothes are sweaters, mufflers, pullovers, caps and socks. We get wool from animals like lambs, sheep, camels, goats, yaks and rabbits.

In the rainy season, people wear raincoats or use umbrellas.

Different Clothes in Different Seasons

Traditional Clothes

Different countries have different traditional dresses. People wear traditional clothes on particular occasions.

Japan

India

Saudi Arabia

Ireland

China

DIFFERENT UNIFORMS

Uniforms are special clothes to show that some people are different from other

people. People wear uniforms according to their work. For example, school uniform

Doctor

Nurse

Police

Student

Nowadays there are varieties of modern clothes. We look different and smart when we wear modern clothes. Above all, it is a healthy habit to wear clean clothes.

THINGS YOU SHOULD DO

- ✓ We should wear clean clothes every day.
- ✓ We should wash our clothes regularly.
- ✓ We should choose good clothes to look smart.
- ✓ We should not wear dirty clothes.
- ✓ We should cover ourselves properly in the winter season.
- ✓ We should not play in rainwater puddles as we may fall ill.

Summary of the Chapter

- We wear clothes to cover our bodies.
- We wear cotton clothes in summer.
- We wear raincoats in the rainy season.
- We get cotton from cotton plants.
- We wear woollen clothes in winter.
- People wear different clothes in different countries.
- People wear uniforms according to their work.

Words to Know

Uniform: Special clothes that a person wears according to his/her work
Traditional Clothes: Regional clothes
Modern Clothes: Fashionable clothes

A. Fill up the blanks.

1. In ancient times, people covered their bodies with .... and ....
2. Clothes protect us from ...., ... and ....
3. Modern people wear .... clothes.
4. Different countries have different .... clothes.
5. In summer, people wear .... clothes.
6. We get cotton from .... plants.

B. Write **T** for a true statement and **F** for a false one.

1. Clothes protect us from the sun.
2. We get wool from plants.
3. We get leather from animals.
4. We use raincoats in the rainy season.
5. We wear woollen clothes in summer.
6. We wear cotton clothes in the winter season.

C. Match the columns.

Column A	Column B
1. Summer	a. Woollen clothes
2. Winter	b. Fine clothes
3. Rainy season	c. Cotton clothes
4. School	d. Raincoat
5. Wedding	e. Uniform

D. Answer these questions.

1. Why do people wear different types of clothes?
2. Who were called aboriginals?
3. What is a uniform? Name some persons who wear uniforms.

4. Why do we wear cotton clothes in summer?

5. Why do we wear woollen clothes in winter?

A. Paste the pictures of the different types of clothes on a chart paper and label them. Bring the chart to the class and paste it on the wall.

B. Colour this picture beautifully.

You are going for a birthday party. You don't like the dress your mother has chosen for you to wear.

Will you:

- refuse to wear the dress and wear the dress you want to?

- grumble a bit, but finally wear the dress your mother has chosen?

- wear the dress your mother has chosen, but tell her that the next time you will choose your own dress?

- wear the dress your mother has chosen without saying anything?

My Family

- Types of Families
- Names and Surnames
- Role of the Family
- Things You Should Do

> "You don't choose your family. They are God's gift to you, as you are to them."
>
> – Desmond Titu

SPOTLIGHT

- Sharing and caring brings happiness to the family.

The people who live together in a house are called a family. Grandparents, parents, uncles, aunts and children together make a family. It is a group of people who are related to one another.

TYPES OF FAMILIES

There are different types of families. Some are large and some are small.

Nuclear Family

A nuclear family has a father, a mother and one or two children. Such family is also called a small family.

Family

Large Family

A family which includes a father, a mother and their three or more children is called a large family.

Joint Family

A family in which parents, grandparents, uncles, aunts and cousins live together under one roof is called a joint family.

Single-Parent Family

A family where children are brought up by either the father or the mother is called a single-parent family.

Nuclear Family

Joint Family

Large Family

NAMES AND SURNAMES

You always see that a person's name has two parts. One is its given name, like Ankit. The other is the surname, like Sharma.

Your surname is your family name. Everyone in your family will have different names, but the same surname.

ROLE OF THE FAMILY

We are different units of a family. A family cannot stand alone. So, we live together. Each member of the family has a special role. When we feel sick, our parents take care of us. Our parents also help us in studies. Sometimes they also play with us. Our grandparents tell us funny and interesting stories. Children also show their love for the family by helping them at home.

THINGS YOU SHOULD DO

✓ You should obey your parents.

✓ You should share work at home.

✓ You should keep your room clean.

✓ You should water plants.

✓ You should not fight against your brothers and sisters.

✓ You should talk politely.

Summary of the Chapter

- Our family consists of parents, brothers and sisters.
- A nuclear family is the one where parents live with their children.
- A joint family is the one where parents, uncles, aunts, cousins and grandparents live together.
- Each member of the family has a special role.

Words to Know

Nuclear family: A family that consists of parents and children

Cousins: Children of uncles and aunts

Joint family: A family in which grandparents, parents, aunts and cousins live together

Uncles: Brothers of parents

Evaluation Time

A. Tick (✓) the correct options.

1. In a .... family, children live with either the father or mother.

   a. single-parent ☐   b. small ☐   c. joint ☐

2. A group of people related to one another is a ....

   a. family ☐   b. surname ☐   c. none of these ☐

3. In a .... family, grandparents, uncles, aunts and parents live together.

   a. big ☐   b. small ☐   c. joint ☐

23

4. Seema and Reema are twins. They may be called ....
   a. brothers ☐   b. sisters ☐   c. siblings ☐

B. Fill up the blanks.

1. In a nuclear family, parents live with their ....
2. The people who live together in a house are called a ....
3. When we feel sick, our .... take care of us.
4. Your surname is .... name .
5. Every member of the family has a .... role.
6. The children (brother and sister) of the same parents are called
    ....
7. We should obey our ....

C. Write **T** for a true statement and **F** for a false one.

1. A family cannot stand alone. ☐
2. We live together in a school. ☐
3. A joint family is a small family. ☐
4. We should not keep our room clean. ☐
5. A family consists of parents, brothers and sisters. ☐
6. We should not fight against our brothers and sisters. ☐

D. Give the name of the person who does the following for you.

1. She takes care of me   ....
2. He goes to office   ....
3. She is my uncle's daughter   ....
4. I play with him   ....
5. She tells me stories   ....

E. Answer these questions.

1. What is a single-parent family?
2. What is a nuclear family?

3.   What should be the role of each member of a family?

4.   What is a joint family?

Recreation Time

A.   Paste the photographs of the members of your family, write their names and make your own family album. Write one sentence about each member.

B.   Get a picture of your pet animal. Talk about it in the class. What does it eat? Discuss.

Circle of Life

You have a little sister. Which of the following things should you do to make her feel happy?

- Buy chocolate
- Give a toy
- Cut jokes
- Tease her
- Play with her

5 Our Shelters

It's a privilege to wake up in this house that existed before us, and will exist after us.

— Tim Cuppett

SPOTLIGHT

- Each of us needs a house to live-in, in order to relax comfortably.

Long, long ago, early men lived in caves. Later, they started building houses with mud, straw, wood, stones and bricks.

Early men lived in caves.

An ancient house

A house is a place where we live. Birds live in nests and animals live in natural or man-made shelters. People live in houses. Our houses protect us from heat, cold and rain. They also protect us from danger and harm.

TYPES OF HOUSES

There are two types of houses – Kutcha houses and Pucca houses.

Kutcha House

Kutcha houses are made up of wood, mud, leaves and straw. They are called huts. Many people in villages live in huts. Such houses are commonly found in villages.

Pucca House

Some people live in pucca houses. These houses are made of bricks, cement, wood and steel. Such houses are found in towns and cities.

Kutcha House

Pucca House

Bungalows are mostly found in towns and cities. A bungalow is one-or two-storeyed house. It is a large house with a lawn.

In some big cities like Delhi, Mumbai, Chennai and Kolkata, people live in flats. High-rise buildings are called Skyscrapers. Such buildings have parks, shops, clubs and swimming pools as well.

Bungalow

Skyscrappers

Stilt house

Stilt houses are built on high bamboo poles (stilts); we find them in places with heavy rainfall.

Some people live in Kashmir in **house-boats**. These houses float on water. They can be taken from one place to another.

Caravan

A **caravan** is a house on wheels. It can move from one place to another.

Igloos are houses made of snow. They are built in extremely cold places. People living in igloos are called **Inuits (Eskimos)**.

Igloo

We should keep our houses clean and tidy. We should place all things at their proper places. We should grow plants and trees around our houses.

Summary of the Chapter

- Houses protect us from rain, heat and cold.
- There are two types of houses: Pucca house and Kutcha house.
- We must keep our houses clean and tidy.
- We must put all things at their proper places.

Words to Know

Shelter: To protect
Skyscraper: A very tall building

Evaluation Time

A. Tick (✓) the right option.

1. The early men lived in:

   a. tent ☐   b. house-boat ☐   c. caves ☐

2. Bungalows are mostly found in:

   a. cities ☐   b. towns ☐   c. both (a) and (b) ☐

3. A house-boat sails on water in:

a. Punjab ☐ b. Kashmir ☐ c. none of these ☐

4. Permanent houses are also called:

a. Kutcha houses ☐ b. Pucca houses ☐ c. None of these ☐

B. Fill up the blanks.

1. A house keeps us safe from ....
2. A house made of wood, stones, mud and straw is a ....
3. A .... is a house on wheels.
4. .... are houses made of snow.
5. We must keep our house .... and ....

C. Write **T** for a true statement and **F** for a false one.

1. Multi-storeyed flats are usually found in villages. ☐
2. A house protects us from danger and harm. ☐
3. A strong house is made of mud. ☐
4. The early humans lived in caves. ☐
5. Houses are of four types. ☐

D. Answer these questions.

1. Why do we need a house?
2. Where do we find pucca houses?
3. What is special about a caravan?
4. What are kutcha houses made of?

Draw a picture of an ideal house on a chart paper.

We should help our parents to keep our house clean. Paste the pictures of three things that you would need to keep your house clean, on a A-4 size sheet.

Services in the Neighbourhood

- Neighbourhood Services
- Things You Should Do

> "Borrow trouble for yourself, if that's your nature; but don't lend it to your neighbours."
>
> – Rudyard Kipling

- Our neighbours are our friends. We help one another in times of need. We share one another's joys and sorrows.

The surroundings around our house are known as the neighbourhood. The people living in our neighbourhood are called neighbours. A good neighbourhood always provides some important services to its people. Some essential services available in the neighbourhood are bank, market, police station, fire station and hospital.

Fire Station

Market

Hospital

NEIGHBOURHOOD SERVICES

Market Complex

A small market is located in our neighbourhood. We buy things of daily use from the market. From grocery shops we buy foodgrains, pulses, vegetables, fruits and cosmetics. We can buy bread, biscuits, cakes, pastries, eggs and cold drinks from the confectioner's shop.

Market Complex

Hospital

A hospital is a very important place in the neighbourhood. When we are seriously sick, we have to go to the hospital. Doctors treat patients and nurses look after them in the hospital. In case of emergency, hospitals send ambulances to carry patients.

Hospital

Some neighbourhoods have no hospitals. They have dispensaries. A dispensary is not as big as a hospital. In most villages, doctors run private clinics in their homes. These private clinics are known as dispensaries.

Post Office

Our neighbourhood has a post office. It is an important means of communication. We can send letters and parcels through a post office. We get stamps, postcards and stamped envelopes there. We can also send parcels and money orders from a post office. There is also a letterbox kept near our house. The postman collects all the letters and takes them to the post office. From there, the letters are sent to different destinations.

Post Office

Nowadays postal insurance is introduced. People keep money in the post office for safety.

Banks

There is a bank in our neighbourhood. We can keep our money and jewellery in

the bank. They are safe there. We can take them out when we need them. We can also deposit cheques in the bank. Most of the families in our neighbourhood have accounts with the bank. It is a very useful service in the neighbourhood.

Bank

Police Station

We have a police station in our neighbourhood. The police guard the neighbourhood and keep us safe. They also help us to search for the lost people or things. So, they are our great friends. We must help the police. It is important to remember that should we should dial 100 to get help from the police.

Police Station

Fire Station

A fire station is a very significant place in the neighbourhood. It has fire engines and firemen. Fire engines are also called firebrigades. If there is a fire, they come and help us to put out the fire. We must dial 101 to call up the fire station.

Fire Station

School

A school is a very useful service in a neighbourhood so that children may not have to travel far. Children go to school to read, write and learn many things. They also learn good habits and manners in school. The school is our second home.

School

THINGS YOU SHOULD DO

- ✓ We should keep our neighbourhood places clean.
- ✓ We should go to hospital when we are sick.
- ✓ We should dial 100 and call up the police when we are in danger.

 We should dial 101 when there is fire.

We should dial 102 when we need an ambulance.

We should keep money in a bank for safety.

Summary of the Chapter

- The places near our neighbourhood are called neighbourhood places.
- The main neighbourhood places are: market complex, hospital, fire station, police station and post office.
- A police station has policemen who protect people from danger.
- A hospital has doctors and nurses who treat patients.
- A fire station has firemen who save people from fire.

Words to Know

Market: It is a shopping place.
Ambulance: It is a vehicle which takes patients to the hospital in emergency.
Dispensary: It is a small clinic.
Fire Station: It has firemen to help people who call up to put out fire.

A. Fill up the blanks.

1. A market has many ....
2. To call the police, we dial ....
3. When we are sick, we go to ....
4. In case of a fire, we call the ....
5. The postman collects letters from the ....

B. Write T for a true statement and F for a false one.

1. A fire station has many firemen.
2. Doctors give us toys.

3. If there is a robbery, we call up the fire brigade. ☐

4. We can send letters and parcels through a post office. ☐

5. We buy dolls from the hospital. ☐

C. Match Column A with Column B.

Column A	Column B
1. Postman	a. look after patients.
2. Fire brigade	b. sells different things.
3. Shopkeeper	c. guards the neighbourhood.
4. Policeman	d. puts out fire.
5. Doctors	e. delivers letters and parcels.

D. Answer these questions.

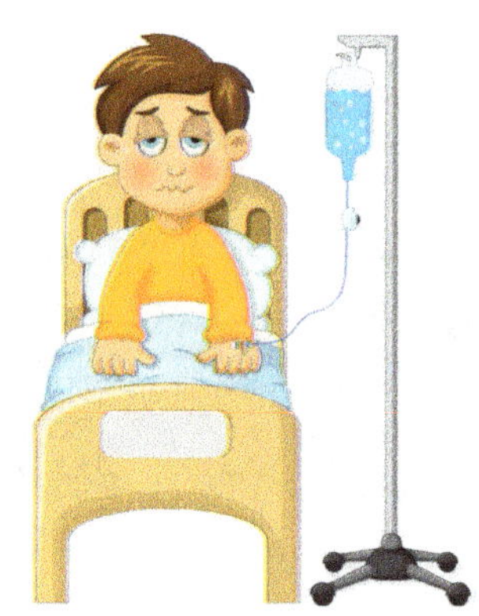

1. What is the role of a bank?

2. Why is a post office useful to us?

3. How do policemen help us?

4. What is the importance of a hospital?

A. Make a neighbourhood diary and collect the phone numbers of your nearest shop, police station, doctor, hospital, bank and post office, and record in the diary.

B. Visit the nearby health clinic. Meet the nurse and the doctor. Write four lines about them.

....

....

....

Always be good to your neighbours. Write five lines about what you should do for your neighbours.

7 Places of Worship

"Anything you do that brings pleasure to God is an act of worship." – John Piper

SPOTLIGHT

- Worship is the way to thank God for the things He has given us.

People worship God in different places. These are called places of worship.

PLACES OF WORSHIP

Temple

The Hindus pray in a temple. Temples have the idols of different gods and goddesses. The Hindus worship many gods and goddesses. The pujari of a temple performs puja. People offer sweets and flowers to the gods and the goddesses. The Ramayana and the Bhagavad Gita are the two holy books of the Hindus.

Temple

Mosques

Jama Masjid

The Muslims pray in a mosque. Islam is the religion of the Muslims. The Muslims offer Namaz, five times a day. The Quran is their holy book. It is based on the belief of one God, Allah. Prophet Muhammad is the founder of Islam.

Gurdwara

The place of worship of the Sikhs is Gurdwara. Their holy book is the Guru Granth Sahib. They pray to their Gurus. Guru Nanakji is the first Guru and founder of Sikhism. The Sikhs celebrate the birthdays of their Gurus as Guru Nanak Jayanti and Gurpurab. The Golden Temple in Amritsar is the most important of all the Gurdwaras. The common kitchen called *langar* in each and every Gurdwara is very popular.

Gurdwara

Church

The place of worship of the Christians is called Church. The Bible is the holy book of the Christians. Jesus Christ is the founder of Christianity. Christmas and Easter are the two important festivals of the Christians.

Church

OTHER PLACES OF WORSHIP

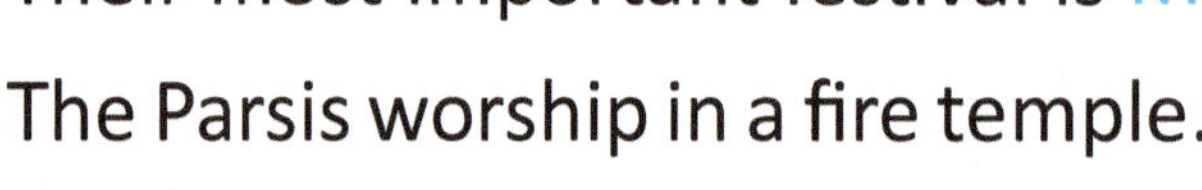

The Buddhists and the Jains also pray in temples. The holy book of the Buddhists is the Tripitaka and the holy books of the Jains are called Angas and Purvas. Their most important festival is Mahavir Jayanti.

Mahavir

The Parsis worship in a fire temple.

So, we see that there are many places of worship for the people of different religions. However, there is only one God, the Almighty God. All religions say the same thing. We are the children of one God.

Jain Shrine

So, we should be good, truthful and loving to one another.

THINGS WE SHOULD DO

✓ We should respect all religions.

✓ We should be truthful.

✓ We should love all.

✓ We should be peaceful.

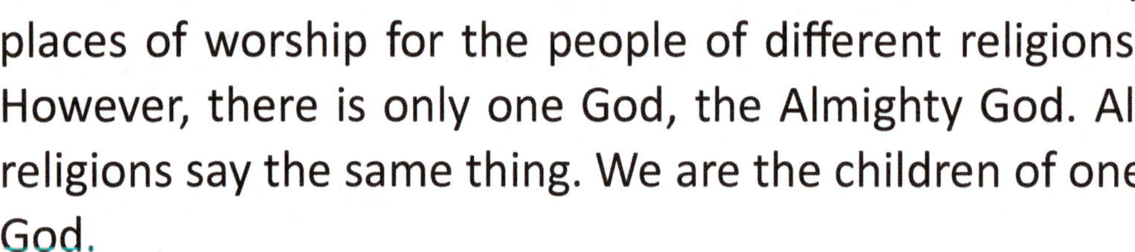

Summary of the Chapter

- People offer prayers in the different places of worship.
- The Hindus pray in temples.
- The Muslims pray in mosques.
- The Sikhs offer prayers in gurdwaras.
- The Christians offer prayers in churches.
- The Buddhists and the Jains pray in their temples.
- The Parsis pray in the fire temple.

Words to Know

Temple: The place of worship of the Hindus
Mosque: The place of worship of the Muslims
Gurdwara: The place of worship of the Sikhs
Church: The place of worship of the Christians

Evaluation Time

A. Fill in the blanks.

1. The Muslims go to a mosque to offer ....
2. A gurdwara is a place of ....
3. A temple has .... of many gods and goddesses.
4. We should .... all religions.
5. .... was the first Sikh Guru.

B. Write T for a true statement and F for a false one.

1. The Bible is the holy book of the Muslims.
2. The Muslims offer prayers in the form of Namaz.
3. The holy book of the Hindus is Tripitaka.
4. The Parsis pray in the fire temple.
5. The Sikhs go to a church to offer prayer.

C. Match Column A with Column B.

Column A	Column B
1. Golden Temple	a. Mosque
2. Christianity	b. Temple
3. Muslims	c. Jesus Christ
4. Parsis	d. Sikhs
5. Hindus	e. Fire temple

D. Read the following clues and fill up the gaps with the names of the places of worship.

1. The Bhagvad Gita teaches the knowledge of life. ....
2. Jesus teaches – Love is God. ....
3. The Sikhs read the Guru Granth Sahib. ....
4. The Muslims offer Namaz. ....

E. Answer these questions.

1. Write a few lines about how the Hindus pray.
2. Who was the founder of Islam?
3. What are the two holy books of the Hindus?
4. Who was the founder of Christianity?
5. Who is the first Guru of Sikhism?

Visit the Golden Temple at Amritsar and the Jama Masjid in Delhi. Write three sentences on each place of worship. Also, paste their pictures in your scrapbook.

People of all religions are humans. So, explore what should be our motive.

Festivals

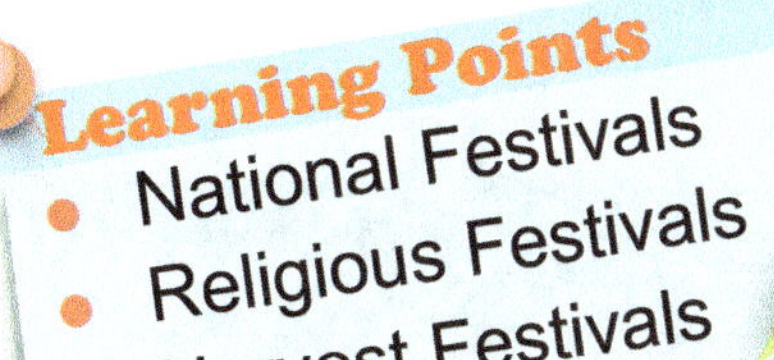

"The greatness of a culture can be found in its festivals."

– Siddharth Katragadda

SPOTLIGHT

- *Festivals are time for fun. They bring us joy and happiness.*

Festivals are special days. People celebrate festivals all over the world. Festivals are a time of joy and happiness. We celebrate them with our family, friends, neighbours and relatives. We greet one another and exchange gifts on most festivals. India is a country of festivals. There are three kinds of festivals celebrated in India - National festivals, Religious festivals and Harvest festivals.

NATIONAL FESTIVALS

A national festival is a festival that is celebrated by the whole country. The National Flag is hoisted and the National Anthem sung on these days. It is a national holiday on each of these festivals.

Independence Day

India became Independent from the British rule on 15th August 1947. We celebrate this day every year as our Independence day. Our Prime Minister hoists the National Flag at the Red Fort in Delhi.

Independence Day

Republic Day

India became a democratic republic on 26nd January 1950. Every year, there is a huge, colourful parade in New Delhi at Rajpath to celebrate it. The President of India takes the salute and hoists the National Flag.

Gandhi Jayanti

Mahatma Gandhi is the father of the nation. His birthday, 2th October, is celebrated as Gandhi Jayanti, every year. People visit his Samadhi at Rajghat to offer flowers and prayers.

Republic Day

Gandhi Jayanti

RELIGIOUS FESTIVALS

People of different religions live together in India. People of all religions have their special days which are called religious festivals.

Diwali

Diwali is an important festival of the Hindus. It is called the festival of lights. Lord Rama returned to Ayodhya after living in a forest for fourteen years on this day. People clean and decorate their houses with diyas (earthen lamps) and candles to welcome Lakshmi, the goddess of wealth. They also wear new clothes and distribute sweets.

Diwali

- We celebrate the different types of festivals in India: religious, national and harvest festivals.
- Religious festivals include Diwali, Id, Christmas, Gurpurab, etc.
- National festivals include Republic Day, Independence Day and Gandhi Jayanti.
- Harvest festivals include Lohri, Onam, Pongal, Bihu, etc.

Words to Know

Harvest Festivals: Festivals celebrated at harvest time
National Festivals: Festivals celebrated by all the people of the nation
Religious Festivals: Festivals celebrated by the people of different religions

Evaluation Time

A. Tick (✓) the right option.

1. On Bihu, we make a sweet called ....

   a. modak ☐   b. sewain ☐   c. pitha ☐

2. Diwali is called the festival of ....

   a. lights ☐   b. colours ☐   c. none of these ☐

3. Pongal is celebrated by the people of ....

   a. Assam ☐   b. Tamil Nadu ☐   c. Kerala ☐

4. On 15th August, our Prime Minister hoists the National Flag at the ....

   a. India Gate ☐   b. Red Fort ☐   c. Rajghat ☐

5. Holi is a ....

   a. harvest festival ☐   b. national festival ☐   c. religious festival ☐

6. Onam is the harvest festival of ....

   a. Kerala ☐   b. Assam ☐   c. Tamil Nadu ☐

B. Fill up the blanks.

1. Chirstmas is celebrated on ....
2. The festival of lights is ....
3. Independence Day is celebrated on ....
4. Gandhi Jayanti is celebrated on ....
5. Id is celebrated at the end of the .... of fasting.
6. Lohri is the harvest festival of ....
7. People enjoy a common meal called .... at Gurdwara.

C. Match Column A with Column B.

Column A	Column B
1. Lohri	a. Assam
2. Id	b. Diyas (Earthen Lamps)
3. Bihu	c. Punjab
4. Diwali	d. Santa Claus
5. Christmas	e. Sewain

D. Answer these questions.

1. Why do we celebrate harvest festivals?
2. Why is Diwali called the festival of lights?
3. Why do we celebrate Christmas?
4. Name the dishes made by the people of Assam on the occassion of Bihu.
5. What do we do on Independence day?

Find out how Holi is celebrated in the different cities of India. Paste the pictures of it in your scrapbook.

We should attend all festivals. Should we make fun of anybody's festival?

9 Our School

- Kinds of Schools
- Things We Learn at School
- Helpers at School
- Good Manners in School
- Things We Should Do

"For everyone of us who succeeds, it is because there's somebody there to show you the way out. The light doesn't always necessarily have to be in your family; for me it was teachers and school." — Opran Winerty

SPOTLIGHT

- A school is a place where people go to learn about topics like reading and writing. In a school, teachers help students to learn.

We all go to school. It is a place where we learn many things. A child who goes to school is called a student or a pupil.

Some children go to school in their neighbourhood. Some go to schools which are far from their homes. They go by bus or by rickshaw.

KINDS OF SCHOOLS

There are many kinds of schools in our neighbourhood.

A pre-school includes a play school and kindergarten.

Pre-primary School

Pre-schools prepare young children for primary school.

Schools up to class 5 are Primary schools. Schools up to class 8 are Middle schools. Schools up to class 10 are Secondary schools. Schools up to class 12 are Senior Secondary schools.

The school has an assembly hall. It has a big playground with slides, swings and see-saws.

Primary School

THINGS WE LEARN AT SCHOOL

We learn many things at school. We learn to read and write. We learn to do sums to paint and to draw. We also learn about our world. We also learn to become good children.

HELPERS AT SCHOOL

The Principal is the head of the school. She/He takes care of the whole school There are many teachers and helpers in the school.

Principal

Teacher

Librarian

Gardener

Guard

Peon

Helpers do many things for us. We must thank them to help us.

GOOD MANNERS IN SCHOOL

Our good manners show that we care for others. We must keep our classroom and our school

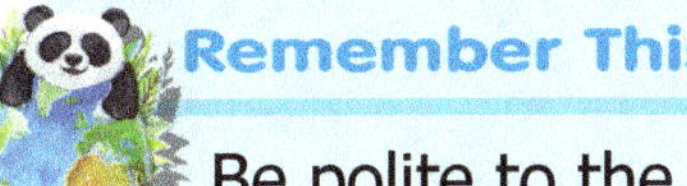

clean. We must not make a noise in the class. We must not scratch our desks or write on walls. We should always throw garbage in the dustbin. We must be polite to all children and teachers. We must not spoil plants and trees in our school.

THINGS WE SHOULD DO

- ✓ We should go to shcool in time.
- ✓ We should obey our teachers.
- ✓ We should prepare our lessons well.
- ✓ We should not quarrel in the class.
- ✓ We should send an application for leave.
- ✓ We should play fair games.
- ✓ We should not tell lies in the class.
- ✓ We should not cheat in the class.
- ✓ We should be polite and obedient.

Summary of the Chapter

- We learn many things at school.
- There are many people who work in school like principal, teacher, librarian, gardener, peon, etc.
- Be polite to the people who help you in school.

Words to Know

Primary: School of education for children below the age of 11
Principal: The head of school
Kindergarten: The school for very small children

A. Tick (✓) the right option.

1. The head of the school is ....

    a. Principal ☐   b. Clerk ☐   c. Teacher ☐

2. Schools up to class 5 are ....

    a. Primary schools ☐   b. Middle schools ☐

    c. Secondary schools ☐

3. Schools up to class 8 are ....

    a. Primary schools ☐   b. Middle schools ☐

    c. Secondary schools ☐

4. Schools up to class 12 are ....

    a. Middle schools ☐   b. Secondary schools ☐

    c. Senior Secondary schools ☐

B. Fill up the blanks.

1. The child who goes to school is called a ....

2. The .... is the head of the school.

3. We must .... helpers to help us.

4. We must keep our school .... and clean.

C. Write 'T' for a true statement and 'F' for a false one.

1. We should respect and obey our teachers. ☐

2. We should scratch our desks or write on walls. ☐

3. We should keep our classroom clean. ☐

4. We should spoil plants and trees. ☐

5. A primary school is from classes I to V. ☐

D. Answer these questions.

1. What do you learn in your school?

2. What is the head of a school called?

3. Is your school a Secondary school or a Senior Secondary school?

4. Name any four school helpers.

5. Write any three duties of a student.

Paste and write the names of the things you carry in the school, in your scrapbook.

Suppose you are the monitor of your class. Write the rules of conduct your classmates should abide by.

10 Weather and Seasons

- Different Seasons in our Country

"Winter is an etching, spring a water colour, summer an oil painting and autumn a mosaic of them all."

– Stantey Horowitz

SPOTLIGHT

- Weather changes every month. Some months are cold and some are hot.

The words windy, sunny, chilly and cloudy describe weather. The weather is the condition of the air around us. It may change during the same day or over a few days. Change in weather is caused by the sun, wind, clouds and rain.

When a place has the same weather for a long time, it is known as the climate of a place.

When the weather remains the same for a few months, we call it a season. There are four seasons throughout the world: Spring, Summer, Autumn and Winter. In our country, there are five main seasons: Summer, Monsoon, Autumn, Winter and Spring.

Cool Weather

DIFFERENT SEASONS IN OUR COUNTRY

Summer

In summer, the sun shines very brightly and it is very hot. The summer months in most places in our country are April, May and June. The sun is the hottest and brightest during these months. We wear cotton clothes and drink chilled drinks like lassi (buttermilk), shakes and juices. Fans, desert coolers and air conditioners are used everywhere.

Summer

Monsoon

Monsoon

The rainy season is called monsoon in India. The rain brings relief after the hot summer.

The monsoon months are July, August and September. Ponds, lakes and rivers get filled up with water. In some places, the monsoon starts in June itself. We use umbrellas or wear raincoats and gumboots when we go out. They protect us from rain. Farmers wait for the monsoon. They need water for their crops. Sometimes we see a rainbow in the sky on a rainy day.

Winter

We feel cold in winter. Cold winds blow and a blanket of fog descends upon the earth. We wear woollen clothes and use blankets and quilts to keep ourselves warm. People light fires or use heaters to keep warm. Winter lasts from November till February. December and January are the coldest months in India.

Winter

Spring

The spring months are February and March. It is the season of joy. During this season, it is neither too hot nor too cold. Flowers are in full bloom and birds chirp. In this season, weather is very pleasant.

Autumn

Autumn comes after monsoon and before winter. The autumn months are September and October. It is dry and windy. Dry leaves fall from trees.

Spring

Autumn

Summary of the Chapter

- There are five seasons in India.
- Summer is the hottest season.
- December and January are the coldest months in India.
- Monsoon is the rainy season.

Words to Know

Monsoon: Rainy season in India
Season: The weather over a long period of time
Weather: The change in the air of a place

A. Tick (✓) the right option.

1. The weather of a place may change on ....
   a. daily basis ☐   b. few days ☐   c. month to month ☐
2. .... is the hottest time of the year.
   a. Summer ☐   b. Winter ☐   c. Monsoon ☐
3. We wear woollen clothes in ....
   a. summer ☐   b. winter ☐   c. monsoon ☐
4. We use umbrellas or wear raincoats in ....
   a. summer ☐   b. winter ☐   c. monsoon ☐
5. We wear cotton clothes in ....
   a. summer ☐   b. winter ☐   c. monsoon ☐
6. Which is the coldest month in India?
   a. March ☐   b. December ☐   c. February ☐

B. Fill up the blanks.

1. When one type of weather continues for many days, we call it a ....
2. .... is the hottest time of the year.
3. We wear woollen clothes in ....
4. The weather in spring is ....
5. Sometimes we see a colourful .... in the sky on a rainy day.
6. .... and .... are the coldest months in India.
7. The rainy season is called .... in India.
8. We wear .... clothes during the summer season.

C. Write T for a true statement and F for a false one.

1. Farmers need water for their crops. ☐
2. We wear cotton clothes in winter. ☐
3. We use a heater in the spring season. ☐
4. October is an autumn month. ☐

5. Spring is the season of joy.

6. Autumn is a dry and windy season.

7. Fans, desert coolers and air conditioners are used in winter.

8. In autumn, weather is very pleasant.

D. Match the columns.

Column A	Column B
1. January	a. summer
2. March	b. monsoon
3. May	c. winter
4. July	d. autumn
5. October	e. spring

E. Answer these questions.

1. What is weather?
2. Name the five seasons of India.
3. What type of weather do we have in summer?
4. Which are the coldest months in India?
5. Which months have rainfall in India?
6. Which months have the spring season?
7. Which months have the autumn season?

Make a scrapbook of all the seasons we have in India. For the summer season, paste the pictures of fruits and vegetables.

An orphan girl comes to you for help in the month of winter. What should you give her to protect her from cold?

11 Rest and Recreation

"Your calm mind is the ultimate weapon against your challenges. So, relax."

– Bryant Mc Gill

SPOTLIGHT

- A circus is an old and popular means of recreation. Clowns, trapeze-artists and acrobats perform in a circus. People enjoy watching them.

After our work or study, we get tired. So, we need rest. We also need to have fun in our free time. When we have fun, we enjoy things. This is called recreation. We feel relaxed in our free time. After taking rest, we feel fresh and good.

RECREATIONAL ACTIVITIES

Any kind of activity in free time is good for recreation if you enjoy it. For example, some children like to enjoy cartoon films on television. Some children like to see puppet shows.

Some children like to play indoor games such as ludo, carrom and chess. Some like to play outdoor games such as football, cricket or badminton as recreation. Outdoor games keep us fit and healthy.

Puppet Shows

Some children like to read books in the library. Reading is a very good habit. We should read good books.

Sometimes people listen to music in their free time. It refreshes their minds.

Some children like to play on swings, see-saws and slides. They enjoy and have fun in the park.

Some children like to go on a picnic in the neighbourhood. Some like to go to the zoo. Some children like to go to village fairs along with their parents.

Recreation in Park

Fair

Drawing and painting are also very good forms of recreation. Some people find cooking very enjoyable.

So, it is important to have free time. It helps to avoid feeling tired and dull. Recreation always makes us feel cheerful. We should all have some recreational activities.

Summary of the Chapter

- There are many things for recreation such as playing, singing, painting, swimming, etc.
- Any kind of activity in free time is good for recreation.
- Recreation always makes us feel cheerful.

Words to Know

Leisure: Spare time or time when one is not working.
Recreation: What we do in our free time for enjoyment.

Evaluation Time

A. Tick (✔) the right option.

1. We play this game in the school playground.

   a. Cricket ☐   b. Ludo ☐   c. Carrom ☐

2. We play it inside the house.

   a. Hockey ☐   b. Chess ☐   c. Football ☐

3. Clowns, trapeze-artists and acrobats perform in the:

   a. circus ☐   b. puppet show ☐   c. movie ☐

4. A good way to spend free time:

   a. fighting ☐   b. sleeping ☐   c. reading books ☐

B. Fill up the blanks.

1. When we have fun, we enjoy things. This is called ....

2. Outdoor games keep us .... and ....

3. .... is a very good habit.

4. .... and .... are also very good forms of recreation.

C. Write 'T' for a true statement and 'F' for a false one.

1. We must do things we enjoy. ☐

2. The games we play outside the house are called indoor games. ☐

3. There are swings and see-saws in the park. ☐

4. Drawing is a good form of recreation. ☐

5. Recreation is always boring. ☐

D. Answer these questions.

1. What is an indoor game?

2. Name three indoor games.

3. What do you see in the park?

4. Where do you go in your holidays?

5. What do you like to do in your free time?

6. How does an outdoor game help us?

7. Why do you need rest?

8. Name some recreational activities.

A. Look at the pictures below. Tick (✓) the ones that are the forms of recreation and cross (✗) the ones that are not.

B. Collect some pictures of different things that people do for recreation and paste them in your album book.

Organise a puppet show to be performed at your nearest park
Discuss the following.

- When and where should it be held?

- How many children will go there?

- How can you help your handicapped sister to go there?

- What food should you carry with you?

- What should you do after the show?

12 Road Safety

- Road Safety Rules
- Rules While Boarding a Bus
- Rules of Traffic Lights

"Safety awareness should begin from childhood as it is difficult to impart awareness to a grown-up human being."

SPOTLIGHT

- Accidents take place when we are careless. We should be careful at every place.

We have to go out daily for work. While we are on the road, life is not safe. Life on the road is very risky. Many fast-moving vehicles are always seen running on the road. Reckless driving causes road accidents daily. But these accidents can be avoided if we are careful while walking, crossing and driving on the road.

So, let us learn how we can be safe on the road. Safety rules always keep us safe from danger.

ROAD SAFETY RULES

We must follow some rules to be safe on the road.

- You should not play on the road.

Kids crossing the road

- You should not run on the road.
- Always cross a road at the zebra crossing.
- Look at right, then left and then right again while crossing the road.
- Before crossing a road, wait for the traffic to stop.
- Always look at the traffic signal.
- Always cross the road holding your elder's hand.

RULES WHILE BOARDING A BUS

- Do not put your head or hands out of the windows of your school bus or car.
- Do not try to get down from a moving bus.
- Always wait in a **queue** while getting into the bus.

Queue at the Bus Stand

RULES OF TRAFFIC LIGHTS

Have you seen the **traffic lights** on the road?

Do you know what their colours mean?

'**Stop**' says the Red light.

'**Wait**' says the Yellow/Amber light.

'**Go**' says the Green light.

Remember This

William L. Potts invented traffic lights in 1920.

Summary of the Chapter

- We should be careful about road safety.
- We should cross the road only at the zebra crossing.

Words to Know

Reckless: Without thinking or caring that some mishap may occur

Zebra crossing: White-and-black lines drawn on the road that are safe for crossing the road

Traffic lights: A set of red, yellow/amber and green lights for controlling traffic on the road

Evaluation Time

A. Fill up the blanks.

1. We must walk on the ....
2. Use the .... crossing to cross a road.
3. We should not .... while crossing a road.
4. Safety rules keep as safe from ....
5. Life on the road is not ....
6. .... says the Red light.

B. Write T for a true statement and F for a false one.

1. We should play on the road.
2. When many vehicles are coming, cross the road.
3. Get into your school bus one by one.
4. Always cross the road at the zebra crossing.
5. We should not be careful about road safety.

C. Answer these questions.

1. Where is our life risky?
2. What type of driving causes road accidents?
3. Which rules keep us safe?
4. What activity can be dangerous?
5. How should you get into a school bus?
6. What does a traffic light mean?
7. Write five road safety rules.

A. Make a poster on rules for safety on the road. Draw a picture for each rule.

B. Colour the lights correctly and write what each light means.

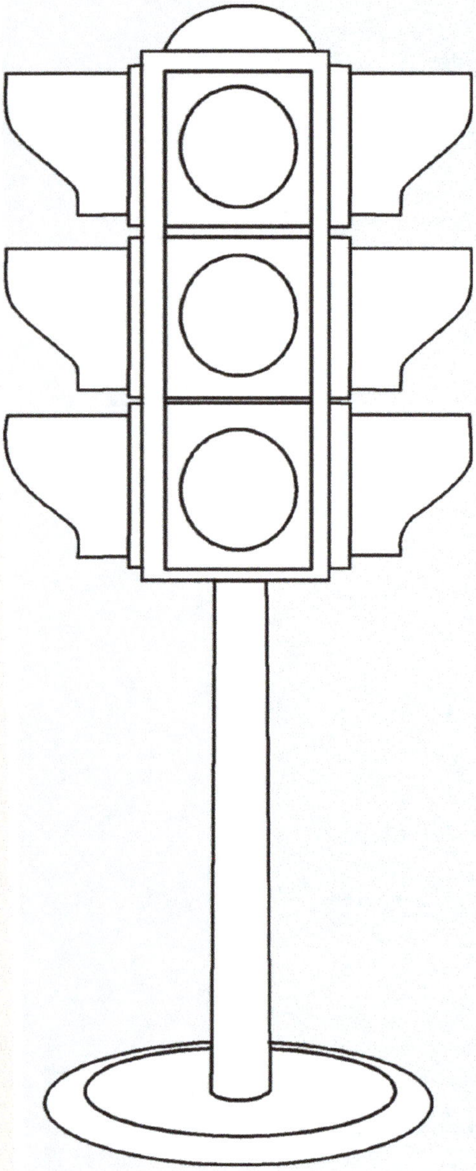

....

....

....

Your friends are playing cricket on the main road. You know it is not safe to do so. But the game looks interesting and you want to join them. What will you do?

- Tell them to continue the game in the park.

- Join them in the game.

- Walk away, but before that ask an adult to stop the children from playing.

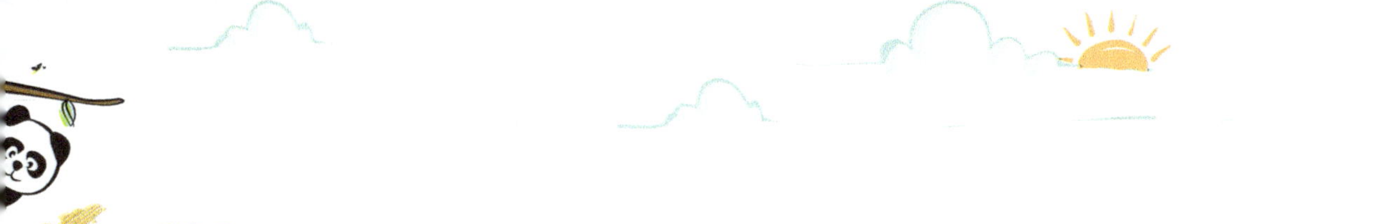

13 Directions and Time

> "The good life is a process, not state of being. It is a direction not a destination."
>
> – Carl Rogers

SPOTLIGHT

- The time just before sunrise is called dawn. The time around sunset is known as dusk.

In the earlier days, people used the sun to find directions. The directions in which the sun rises and sets, never change. The sun rises in the East and sets in the West. When we stand facing sunrise, we are looking towards the East. Behind us is the West where the sun sets. On the left-hand side is the North. The right-hand points to the south.

DIFFERENT DIRECTIONS

We use the words left or right, up or down, behind or in front of and forward or backward to give simple directions. For big areas, we use North, South, East or West.

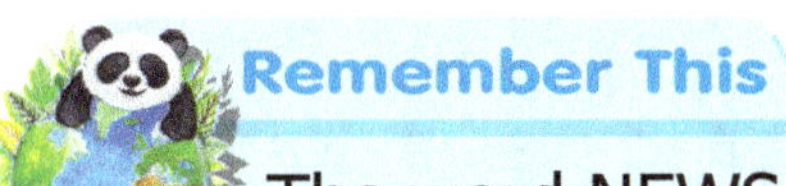

Remember This

The word NEWS is formed of North, East, West and South.

Compass

A sailor uses a compass to find directions. A compass has a needle. It always points in the north direction. The other directions are easily found with its help.

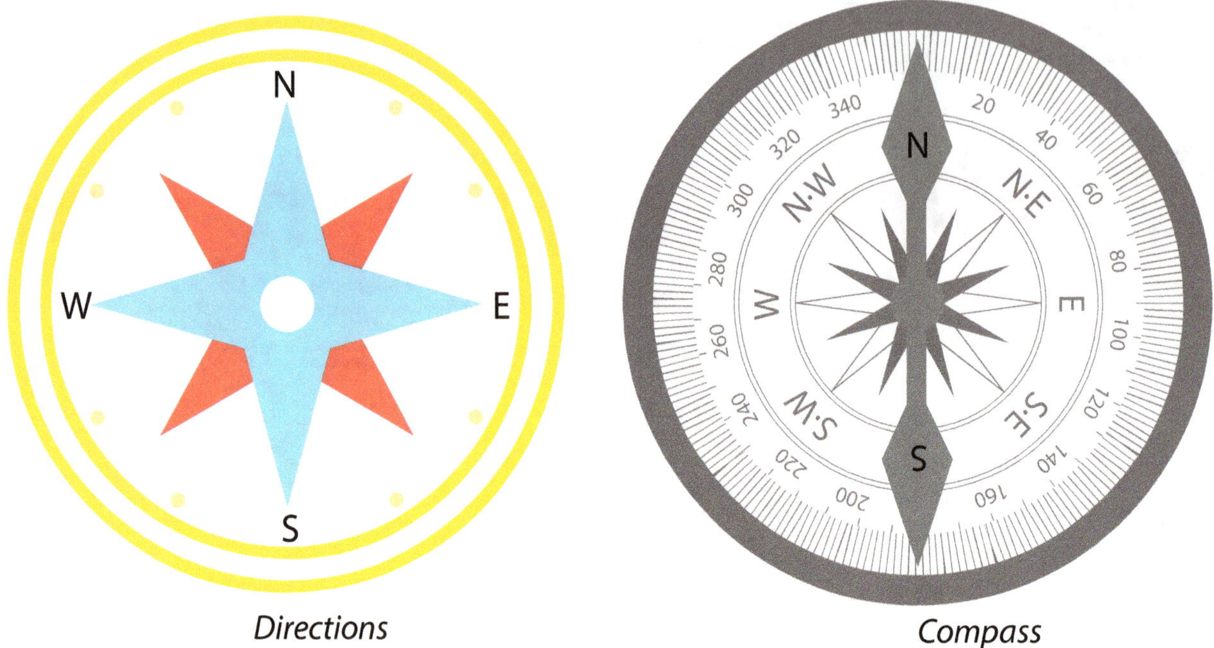

Directions   Compass

Map

When we show the drawings of an area on a piece of paper, we call it a map. It is a diagram or a drawing of a particular area. A map can help us to find out our way if we are in a new place. People travelling by ship also use maps which are called charts.

TIME AND UTILITY OF DIRECTIONS

Time never stands still. The period from sunrise to sunset is called day. The period from sunset to sunrise is called night. A day and night together makes a complete day.

Long, long ago, there were no clocks or watches. During daytime people guessed the time by the position of the sun and the length of the shadow.

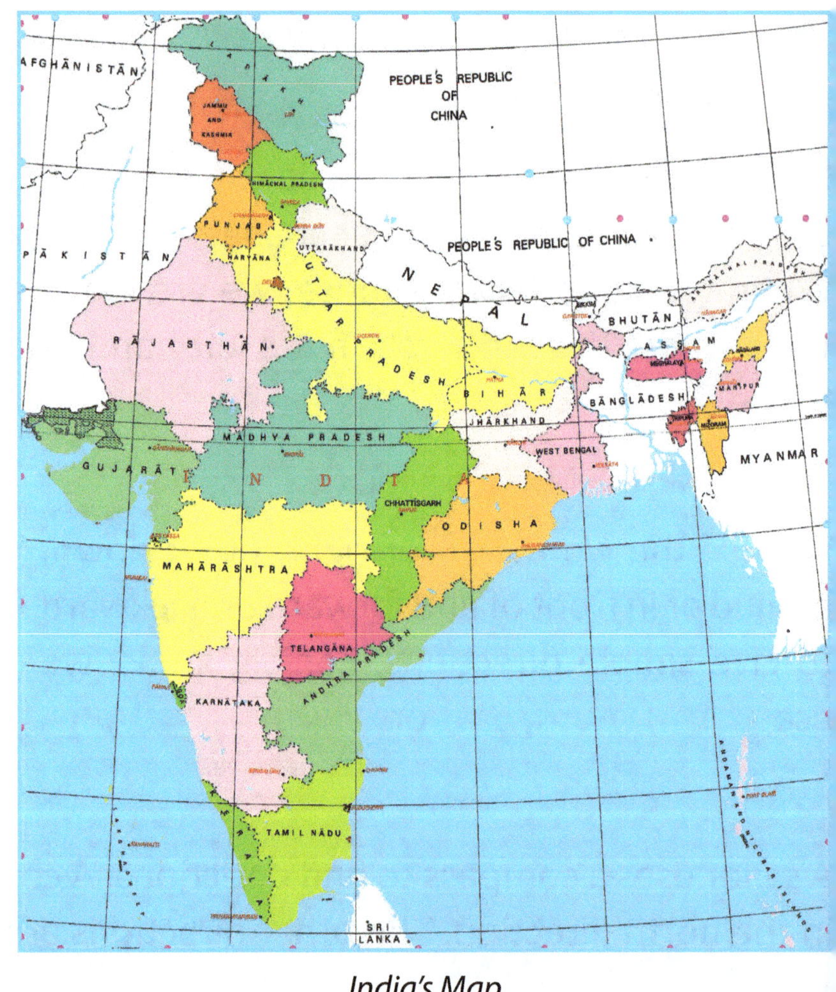

India's Map

Morning

When the sun rises, it is morning. The length of the shadow is long.

Noon

When the sun is above our heads, we call it noon or midday. The time after midday is called afternoon. The length of the shadow is the shortest.

Morning

Noon

Evening

When the sun begins to set, it is evening. Afternoon is followed by evening. The length of the shadow increases.

Evening

Night

Night

When the sun sets completely, it is night. The sky is dark. The moon and the stars appear at night. There is no shadow formed at night.

Hours, Minutes and Seconds

We can measure time in hours, minutes and seconds. We use a clock or watch to know the time.

1 day	=	24 hours
1 hour	=	60 minutes
1 minute	=	60 seconds

Years, Months and Weeks

A calendar shows us the days of the week and the months of the year. Seven days make a week. The seven days of the week are Sunday, Monday, Tuesday, Wednesday, Thursday, Friday and Saturday.

A year has 365 days or 12 months. A month has 30 or 31 days. February has 28 days. In a leap year, it has 29 days. The 12 months in a year are January, February, March, April, May, June, July, August, September, October, November, December.

Summary of the Chapter

- We need to know the directions to find out where a place is.
- East, West, North and South are the main directions.
- The sun rises in the East and sets in the West.
- A day begins in the morning when the sun rises.
- A clock or a watch tells us the time.

Words to Know

Direction: The position of a place or thing
Map: A drawing of a place on paper
Evening: The time when the sun sets
Morning: The time when the sun rises
Noon: 12 o'clock during the day

Evaluation Time

A. Tick (✓) the right option :

1. The sun rises in the ....

   a. East ☐   b. West ☐   c. North ☐

2. A sailor uses a .... to find directions.

   a. map ☐   b. calendar ☐   c. compass ☐

3. A day has .... hours.

   a. 20 ☐   b. 21 ☐   c. 24 ☐

4. A year has ....

   a. 364 days ☐   b. 364 1/4 days ☐   c. 365 days ☐

5. We go to school in the ....

   a. evening ☐   b. morning ☐   c. night ☐

6. One hour is divided into ....

   a. 60 minutes ☐   b. 50 minutes ☐   c. 60 seconds ☐

B. Fill up the blanks.

1. A .... tells us time.

2. The four directions are .... , ... , ... and ....

3. A .... and .... together makes a complete day.

4. We can see the .... and .... at night.

5. The sun rises in the .... and sets in the ....

6. One minute is divided into .... seconds.

C. Write 'T' for a true statement and 'F' for a false one.

1. A clock tells us time. ☐

2. The sun rises in the West. ☐

3. Right and wrong are words related to directions. ☐

4. Our shadow is very short at noon. ☐

5. The period from sunrise is called day. ☐

6. The length of the shadow is the shortest in the morning. ☐

D. Answer these questions.

1. Why do we need to know directions?
2. What is a map?
3. What is a compass?
4. How did people tell the time long, long ago?
5. How do we tell the time now?
6. What do you see in the night sky?

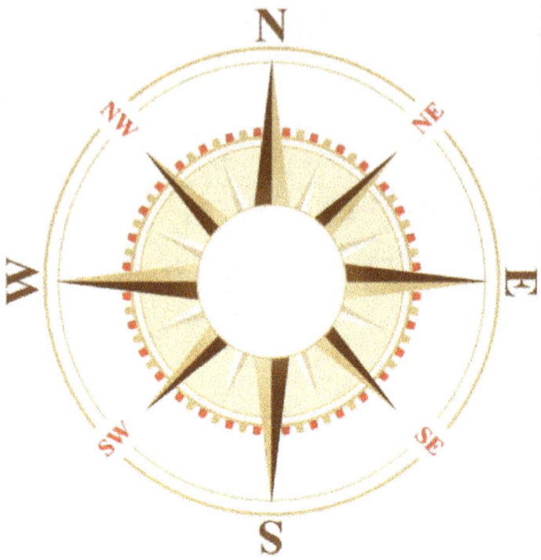

Make a drawing of your house. Find out in which direction the sun rises. Then colour the East red, South green, West yellow and North orange.

Maps are very helpful in finding out different places easily. So, whenever we are going to a place for the first time, we should take the help of a map.

14 Means of Transport

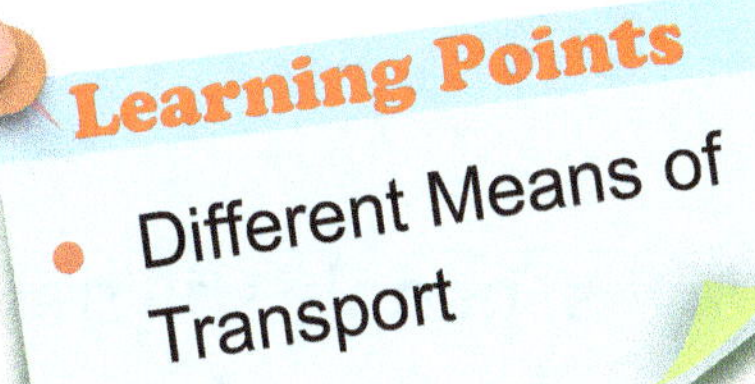

"You can't understand a city without using its transport system."
— Erol O Zam

SPOTLIGHT

- In our daily life we need to go from one place to another for various purposes.

Earlier, people did not have any vehicle. They had to travel on foot or on the back of some animals like horse, camel, ox, etc. Sometimes they used sledges to pull heavy loads. It was difficult to pull a sledge with the load.

Carrying loads on back of animals

One day, the early man saw a round log of wood rolling down the hill. From this he got the idea of the wheel. After the invention of the wheel, the early man used carts to travel. These carts were pulled by animals. Today we have different vehicles to travel on land, water or in the air. These are called means of transport. People can now travel to nearby or far-off places comfortably and easily.

DIFFERENT MEANS OF TRANSPORT

Different means of transport are used in different places.

Roadways

The vehicles that run on the road are called roadways. In villages, people still travel by tongas and bullock-carts. In deserts, people ride on camels, whereas, elephants are used in thick forests. In hills, mules and ponies are used. In cities and towns, people travel by bicycle, rickshaw, scooter, car, bus and train.

Car

Bus

Scooter

Cycle

Rickshaw

Auto-Rickshaw

We travel long distances by train. Trains move on rails. A train has an engine and many coaches. Its engine runs on electricity, coal or diesel. Trains are comfortable and fast. Passenger trains carry people from one place to another. Good trains carry things.

Remember This

The Shatabdi and the Rajdhani trains are super-fast trains in India. They travel at a speed of 200 km per hour.

Waterways

The vehicles that sail on water are called waterways. When we want to cross rivers or seas, we go in a boat steamer or ship. Cargo ships carry heavy loads. Ships, steamers, boats and sailboats are means of water transport. But these are slow means of transport. A ship can take us to very far-off places.

Sailboat

Ship

Steamer

Airways

The vehicles that fly in the air are called airways. When we want to travel long distances in a short time, we go in an aeroplane. It is the fastest means of transport. We can reach other countries in a few hours by air. They also carry goods.

If we want to go somewhere very, very far away, such as the Moon, we can travel in a rocket or spaceshuttle.

Aeroplane

Helicopter

Rocket

Summary of the Chapter

- People have invented many vehicles to move from one place to another.
- Some vehicles are fast and some are slow.
- Some vehicles move on tracks, some on water, some in the air and some on the road.

Words to Know

Fuel: Any substance that produces heat or power when it is burnt
Means of transport: Vehicles used for moving from one place to another
Transporting: Taking things from one place to another

Evaluation Time

A. Tick (✓) the right option.

1. Which vehicle does not have an engine?

   a. scooter ☐   b. auto rickshaw ☐   c. rickshaw ☐

2. We travel very long distances by ....

   a. road ☐   b. air ☐   c. water ☐

3. The vehicles that sail on water are called ....

   a. roadways ☐   b. waterways ☐   c. airways ☐

4. The .... is the fastest means of transport.

   a. bus ☐   b. train ☐   c. aeroplane ☐

5. We go to school by ....

   a. aeroplane ☐   b. bus ☐   c. train ☐

6. In deserts, people use them to travel.

   a. horses ☐   b. camels ☐   c. elephants ☐

B. Fill up the blanks.

1. We can travel long distances over the sea by ....

2. The vehicles that fly in the air are called ....

3. Cargo ships carry heavy ....

4. .... are used in deserts for travelling.

5. The aeroplane is the .... means of transport.

C. Write T for a true statement and F for a false one.

1. My father goes to office by train.
2. We use different means of transport to travel from one place to another.
3. The train moves on rail tracks.
4. Boats and steamers are the means of air transport.
5. The camel is also called 'the ship of the desert'.

D. Name the following.

1. Any three means of water transport

(a) ....   (b) ....   (c) ....

2. Any three means of air transport

(a) ....   (b) ....   (c) ....

3. Any three means of road transport

(a) ....   (b) ....   (c) ....

E. Answer these questions.

1. How did the early man carry his goods?
2. Why do we need the means of transport?
3. In which places are camels used as the means of transport?
4. How are aeroplanes and helicopters useful to us?
5. How can we travel across a sea or an ocean?

Paste the pictures of the different kinds of vehicles in your scrapbook and write their names.

We should not waste fuel. Name two ways in which you can save fuel.

15 Let's Communicate

- Different Means of Communication
- Electronic Means of Communication
- Means of mass Communication

> "The art of communication is the language of leadership."
> – James Humes

SPOTLIGHT

- *Our life has become easier by the use of modern means of communication.*

The world has become a small village due to the various means of communication

Means of communication help us to send our thoughts and feelings. They have made our life better and comfortable. Communication is the act of sending and receiving information from one place to another.

In early days, messengers and pigeons were used for sending and receiving messages

Messenger on horse

Pigeon

DIFFERENT MEANS OF COMMUNICATION

Nowadays there are many latest means of communication. Some of them are given below.

Letters

Letters are very popular and common means of communication. Post cards, inland letters, envelopes are the various types of letters. We buy letters from a post office. We post our letters in the post box.

Post Box

Telegram

A telegram is used for sending short and urgent messages quickly.

Letter

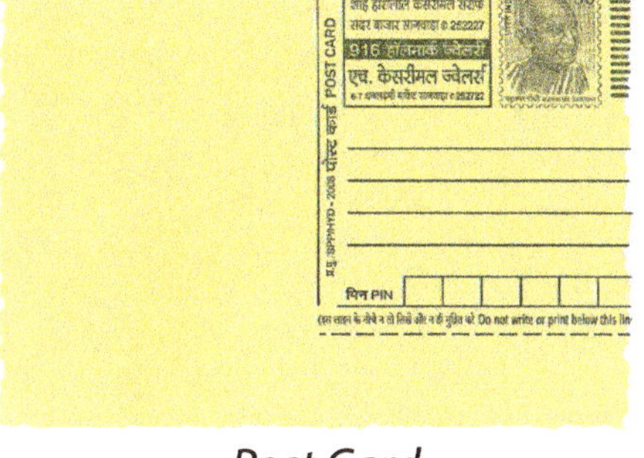

Post Card

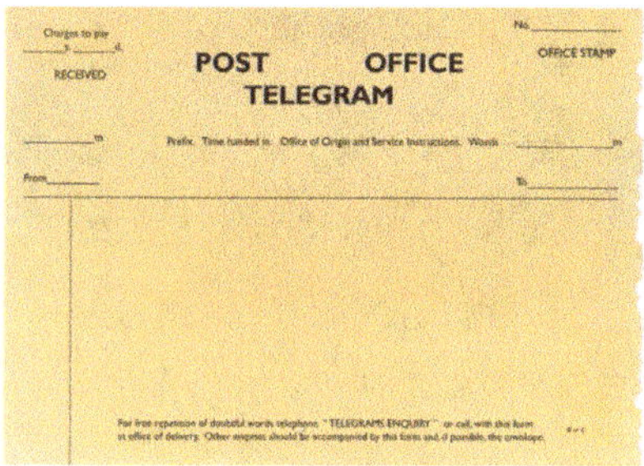

Telegram

ELECTRONIC MEANS OF COMMUNICATION

There are many letters and electronic means of communication. Telephone and mobile phone are the fastest means through which we can directly talk to our friends and relatives.

The Internet is also a very fast means of communication. We can send and receive messages in a few seconds. The Internet is attached through a computer and a mobile phone as well.

Telephone

Mobile Phone

Remember This

The telephone was invented by Alexander Graham Bell.

MASS COMMUNICATION

Newspapers, radio, television, etc. are the means of mass communication. Mass communication means sending the message to a large number of people at one time.

Newspaper

Television

Radio

Summary of the Chapter

- Means of communication help us to send our thoughts and feelings.
- We post our letters in the post box.
- Newspapers, radio, television, etc. are the means of mass communication.
- Nowadays cable network makes it possible to watch 'live' programmes on television.
- In early days, messengers and pigeons were used for sending and receiving messages.
- Urgent letters can be sent through telegrams.

Words to Know

Message: Spoken, written or electronic communication
Messenger: A person who carries a message
Mass: Involving a large number of people or things

Evaluation Time

A. Tick (✓) the right option :

1. We buy a letter from the ....

   a. bank   b. post office   c. shop

2. Which one of the following is used for sending urgent and quick messages?

   a. Telegram ☐   b. Newspaper ☐   c. Letter ☐

3. We talk over the:

   a. telephone ☐   b. radio ☐   c. letter ☐

B. Fill up the blanks :

1. .... and .... are used in early days for communication.
2. The .... is attached through a computer.
3. A telegram is used for sending .... messages.
4. Mobile phones are the .... means of communication.

C. Write **T** for a true statement and **F** for a false one.

1. The ways for communicating with others are called means of transport. ☐
2. Newspapers are the cheapest means of communication. ☐
3. Radio is very useful to those who don't know how to listen. ☐
4. E-mail stands for electrical mail. ☐

D. Answer these questions.

1. What do you mean by communication?
2. Name the different types of letters.
3. What are the electronic means of communication?
4. What do you mean by mass communication?

Read newspapers and write the important news-items of the last week in your notebook.

Name the means of communicaiton you have used.

16 Story of the Wheel

> *"I build engines and attach wheels to them."*
> – Enzo Ferrari

SPOTLIGHT

- The invention of the wheel and discovery of fire are considered the most significant landmarks in the history of human beings.

Long ago, human beings had to walk everywhere. They had to carry their own loads. There were no carts. This was becuase the wheel had not been invented at that time.

THE INVENTION OF THE WHEEL

One day, an early human must have seen a log of wood rolling down a hill. This must have given him the idea of making a wheel.

The first rough wheel must have been a round log of wood.

Loads could be rolled along over several such logs.

Invention of the Wheel

A clever early human must have one day cut two round pieces from a log. He made holes in the centre and passed a stick through the holes. He joined a few more sticks to it to make a cart.

This cart could now be easily pushed or pulled to carry heavy loads.

Use of the Wheel

And so, the wheel was invented! The wheel was one of the most important inventions made by humans. It changed the way humans lived.

USES OF THE WHEEL

Wheels help in transport since the wheel is used in nearly each and every kind of vehicle.

Car

Bus

Wheels are used in most machines, as gears and propellers. The wheel is used for producing energy, for example, in water wheels. The potter's wheel is used for shaping clay.

Potter's wheel

Summary of the Chapter

- The first rough wheels must have been round logs of wood.
- Wheels help in transport.
- The wheel is used for producing energy.

Words to Know

Wheel: Circular object that rolls easily
Several: Many

Evaluation Time

A. Fill up the blanks.

1. Early humans had to .... everywhere.
2. Early humans had to carry their own ....
3. The .... was an important invention.

B. Answer these questions.

1. How did early humans get the idea of the wheel?
2. Describe the first wheels used by early humans.
3. What are the different uses of the wheel?

What kinds of transport do you see in villages today? Make a list.

Can you ride your bicycle without wheels? If there were no wheels, how would go to your school and your granny's house?

Rivers

When snow on high mountains melts, it forms streams and rivers. There are many rivers in India. The Ganga is considered as the holiest river.

Lakes

A lake is a large body of fresh or salty water surrounded by land.

Seas and Oceans

A sea is a large water-body. An ocean is larger than a sea. Both cover more than 70% of the earth's surface. The five major oceans on the earth are – Pacific Ocean, Atlantic Ocean, Indian Ocean, Arctic Ocean and Southern Ocean.

Sea water is salty because the rivers that join the sea carry minerals in them.

All plants and animals need water to live. We need water to drink, bathe, cook and wash clothes. Water is home of many kinds of animals such as fish and crocodiles.

River

Lake

Sea and Ocean

Summary of the Chapter

- The shape of the earth is like an orange.
- The earth has different natural features: plains, hills, mountains, valleys and plateaus.
- Very high hills are called mountains.
- Three-fourths of the earth is covered with water.
- Plains are good for growing crops and fruits.
- Sea water is salty, so we cannot drink it.
- When snow melts in mountains, rivers get formed.

Hill: A small mountain
Plateau: A high land that is flat on top and looks like a table
Lake: Water collected in a large area
Plains: Flat land
Ocean: The largest water-body
Sea: A large water-body with salty water

Evaluation Time

A. Tick (✓) the right option :

1. The shape of the earth is like an ....

   a. apple ☐   b. apricot ☐   c. orange ☐

2. A flat land is called a ....

   a. plain ☐   b. valley ☐   c. mountain ☐

3. Three-fourths of the earth is covered with ....

   a. land ☐   b. water ☐   c. forests ☐

4. We cannot drink sea water as it is ....

   a. salty ☐   b. sweet ☐   c. bitter ☐

5. Plants grow very well in .... as they are fertile.

   a. valleys ☐   b. deserts ☐   c. rivers ☐

B. Fill up the blanks.

1. The earth is surrounded by ....

2. Animals cannot live without ....

3. The low land between two hills is called the ....

4. Sea water is ....

5. There are .... oceans on the earth.

6. An .... is bigger than a sea.

C. Answer these questions.

1. What is the difference between a hill and a mountain?
2. What is a plain?
3. What is a valley?
4. What is a plateau?
5. What shape is the Earth?

A. With the help of clay, make a model of the earth. Colour three-fourths of it blue to depict water bodies, and one-fourth green to depict land.

B. Cut out the pictures of different landforms from magazines. Paste them in your scrapbook. Write the names of the landforms below the pictures.

A. We should love and care for our earth. How can we make the earth greener?

B. Write a slogan 'Save Earth, Save Water' in big letters on an A-4 size sheet.

18 Mother Teresa

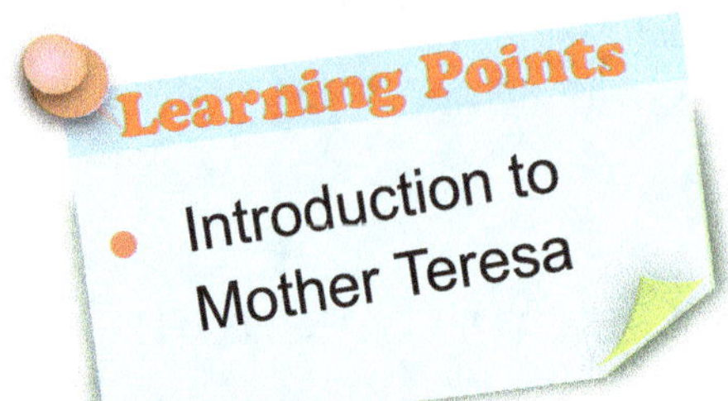

- Introduction to Mother Teresa

"The most terrible poverty is lonliness and the feeling of being unloved." – **Mother Teresa**

SPOTLIGHT

- Mother Teresa was awarded the Nobel Peace Prize and became a symbol of charitable, selfless work.

Mother Teresa was a great Philanthropist. She was born on 26th August 1910 in Skopje (now republic of Macedonia). Her childhood name is Agnes Bojaxhiu. She was a Catholic nun. She came to India to teach in a Convent School in Calcutta (now Kolkata).

Mother Teresa was a great devotee of God. To her, service to man is service to God. She founded Missionaries of Charity to help the poor and the downtrodden.

Mother Teresa also established Shishu Bhavan. It is the house for homeless children (orphans). Her motto was to serve people throughout her life.

Mother Teresa also set up Nirmal Hriday. It was a home for the dying and the poor.

Shishu Bhavan at Kolkata

She looked after every child as a mother. She loved everybody with a pure heart.

In 1979, Mother Teresa was awarded Noble Prize for Peace; in 1980, she got the Bharat Ratna. She breathed her last breath in 1997.

We learn many things from Mother Teresa's life and teachings. The most important of them is to love all from the core of heart.

The Missionaries of Charity is helping more than 125 countries of the world.

The Missionaries of Charity focuses on the following:

- Provide home to the homeless.

- Nurse the sick and the poor.

- Teach the children who cannot go to school.

- Feed millions of hungry people.

Missionaries of Charity

Mother Teresa is a universal mother. She is immortal among us. We pay homage to her departed soul.

Summary of the Chapter

- Mother Teresa was a great philanthropist.
- She established Shishu Bhavan for orphans.
- She was born on 26th August 1910.
- In 1980, she was awarded Bharat Ratna.

Words to Know

Philanthropist: A person who seeks to promote the welfare of others
Orphan: A child who does not have parents

Evaluation Time

A. Fill up the blanks :

1. Mother Teresa's childhood name was ....

2. Shishu Bhavan was a home for homeless ....

3. Mother Teresa taught in a ....

4. Nirmal Hriday is a home for the ....

5. Mother Teresa got Nobel Prize in ....

B. Write T for a true statement and F for a false one.

1. Mother Teresa served animals.

2. Mother Teresa was awarded Bharat Ratna for peace.

3. Mother Teresa was a great devotee of God.

4. Mother Teresa was born on 26th August 1915.

5. Mother Teresa was a Protestant nun.

C. Answer these questions.

1. Who was Mother Teresa?

2. Where was Mother Teresa born?

3. Who established Shishu Bhavan?

4. What does the life of Mother Teresa teach us?

5. What is the role of the Missionaries of Charity?

Get together and make a chart on Mother Teresa. Paste pictures in your scrapbook. Also, write a paragraph about her.

If you see a boy wandering in your street without a shirt or T-shirt on, what will you do for him?